Weapons and Technology

By Martin J. Dougherty

Please visit our Web site www.garethstevens.com. For a free color catalog of all our high-quality books, call toll free 1-800-542-2595 or fax 1-877-542-2596.

Library of Congress Cataloging-in-Publication Data

Dougherty, Martin J.
    Weapons and technology / by Martin J. Dougherty. -- North American ed.
        p. cm. _ (Modern warfare)
    Includes bibliographical references and index.
    ISBN-10: 1-4339-2741-1   ISBN-13: 978-1-4339-2741-6 (lib. bdg.)
    1. Military weapons_Juvenile literature.   2. Weapons systems_Juvenile literature. I. Title.
UF500.D69   2010
623.4_dc22   2009019092

This North American edition first published in 2010 by
Gareth Stevens Publishing
111 East 14th Street, Suite 349
New York, NY 10003

Copyright © 2010 by Amber Books, Ltd.
Produced by Amber Books Ltd., Bradley's Close
74–77 White Lion Street
London N1 9PF, U.K.

Amber Project Editor: James Bennett
Amber Copy Editors: Melanie Gray, Jim Mezzanotte
Amber Designer: Andrew Easton
Amber Picture Research: Terry Forshaw, Natascha Spargo

Gareth Stevens Executive Managing Editor: Lisa M. Herrington
Gareth Stevens Editor: Joann Jovinelly
Gareth Stevens Senior Designer: Keith Plechaty

Interior Images
Kockums: 18 (ThyssenKrupp Marine Systems)
Military Visualizations, Inc.: 1, 11, 20
NASA Dryden Flight Research Centre: 15
Rex Features: 29
U.C. Berkeley: 28
U.S. Department of Defense: 3, 4 (U.S. Air Force), 5, 6, 7 (U.S. Air Force), 8 (both), 9, 10, 12, 13 (NORAD), 14, 16 (U.S. Air Force), 17 (U.S. Air Force), 19 (U.S. Air Force), 21, 22 (U.S. Navy), 23, 24, 25 (U.S. Navy), 26, 27 (U.S. Air Force)

Cover Images
Front cover: U.S. Department of Defense and Eurofighter Typhoon

Printed in the United States of America

CPSIA Compliance Information: Batch #CR011090GS: For further information contact Gareth Stevens, New York, New York at 1-800-542-2595

▶ ROCKET LAUNCH
A Multiple Launch Rocket System
(MLRS) firing a missile.

CONTENTS

CHAPTER 1

SMART WEAPONS

Even in modern warfare, hitting a target is difficult. Some targets are small and hidden. Others may be hard to reach, or may be too close to innocent civilians.

In the past, all weapons were "dumb." Soldiers aimed and fired. Afterward, they had no control. Today, soldiers use "smart" weapons. Computers help control exactly where weapons are fired.

Many smart weapons are missiles. A missile is a small rocket. It travels to the target with its own power.

Remote Control

Some weapons have remote control. A soldier "steers" those weapons with a joystick, similar to playing a video game. The joystick sends a radio signal to steer the weapon.

▼ A "SMART" BOMB
This U.S. A-10 Thunderbolt II attack jet has just dropped a 500-pound (227-kilogram) Paveway II smart bomb. Smart weapons such as the Paveway II are very accurate. They can target a single building or vehicle.

▲ FIRE AND FORGET
Workers in Iraq load a 1000-lb. (454-kg) bomb onto an
F-16 Fighting Falcon. The pilot can "fire and forget"
this bomb. It will steer to the target on its own. The
pilot can focus on returning safely to base.

Controlling remote weapons is a tricky
job. Soldiers need special training. They
must see the weapon and the target at
all times.

Fire-and-Forget Missiles

Some smart missiles find targets on their
own. They are sometimes called "fire-and-
forget" weapons. Soldiers can launch them
and quickly get out of the area.

Some missiles are heat-seeking weapons.
They search for hot targets, such as a fighter
jet's engine. Other missiles use **radar** to locate
targets. Missiles send out radio waves that
bounce back to reveal their location. Those
radio waves outline a picture of the target.

Bombs Get Smart

In the past, pilots dropped bombs and hoped
they hit their targets. Today, bombs are smarter.

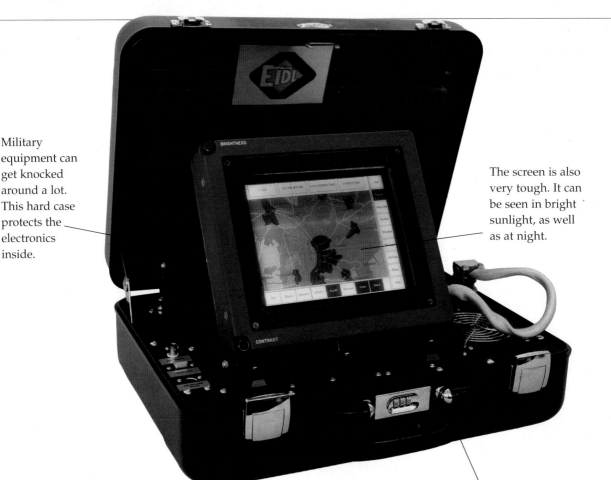

Military equipment can get knocked around a lot. This hard case protects the electronics inside.

The screen is also very tough. It can be seen in bright sunlight, as well as at night.

This GPS unit is easy to carry. Soldiers use it to find smart bombs that have not exploded.

▲ GPS IN A BRIEFCASE
This briefcase contains a military Global Positioning System (GPS) unit. It is similar to the ones used in our cars, but it is much more accurate.

DID YOU KNOW?

The U.S. military created GPS technology. It uses satellites to determine geographic locations. Those tiny spacecraft **orbit**, or circle, Earth. They send signals from space to GPS receivers. Those receivers use the signals to work out exact locations.

They use the **Global Positioning System (GPS)**. It gets signals from space and tells a bomb where to go.

Aim for the Dot

Soldiers also use **lasers** to guide weapons. A laser is a beam of light. It makes a bright dot on the target. The dot guides the weapon.

Laser-guided weapons are very accurate. They can hit small targets. But soldiers must first see the target. They must aim carefully. If the dot moves, the weapon will go off course.

▼ ON THE GROUND

When aircraft drop laser-guided bombs, someone must point the laser at the target. Soldiers on the ground do this job. These soldiers are training to use a laser pointer at a practice range in Nevada.

This U.S. soldier is training to use the laser. He checks the target with binoculars.

This machine is a laser pointer. The soldier points the laser at the target. The smart bomb looks for the laser spot and aims for it.

The soldiers use a radio to talk with the pilots who will drop bombs.

Cruise Missiles

A cruise missile flies long distances. It has a special **navigation** system. That system helps the cruise missile stay on course. It takes off and flies directly to the target. It knows what direction it's heading. It knows how far it has traveled, too.

Cruise missiles also use radar. As they fly, they "see" the ground below. They can recognize hills and buildings along the way.

▲ TESTING A TOMAHAWK
A U.S. submarine launched this Tomahawk Land Attack Missile. The submarine was underwater, 400 miles (644 kilometers) from the target. Tomahawks have jet engines, just like planes. They have wings, too. They can fly more than 1,500 miles (2,414 km).

Sneaky Weapons

Some smart weapons only hit one kind of target, such as tanks. A tank is covered in thick armor, but that armor is often thinner at the top. Missiles are designed to fly over tanks to attack where the armor is thinnest. They may even float down on a parachute. When the missiles detect a tank, they explode.

▼ ANTITANK MISSILE
A soldier gets ready to fire an antitank missile. He points a laser at the tank. The missile follows the laser. It will fly over the tank and then explode over the thin armor on top.

CHAPTER 2

SPACE

Most countries with weapons programs use satellites in outer space. Those satellites help launch and direct weapons. Satellites are useful for other tasks, too. Some can look down on Earth. They show what the enemy is doing. Other satellites enable soldiers to speak with one another, even if they're in different parts of the world.

Getting Into Orbit

If you throw a ball in the air, **gravity** sends it back down. But if you launch something high enough into the sky, it stays up. It goes into orbit, circling Earth.

Great speed is needed to send objects into orbit. Satellites travel in powerful rockets. Those rockets take the satellites into space and then fall away. Space rockets can only be used once. They are usually destroyed when

▶ SPACE ROCKET
An Atlas II rocket carries a satellite for the U.S. Air Force. This kind of rocket can only be used once.

IN THEIR OWN WORDS

"Users everywhere rely on GPS. In 1996, a satellite controller accidentally put the wrong time into one of GPS's 24 satellites. More than 100 cell phone networks on the U.S. East Coast failed."

U.S. Air Force Lt. Gen. Bruce Carlson

▼ EARLY WARNING

The United States and other countries use satellites to watch for enemy missiles being launched. This satellite is part of the U.S. Defense Support Program (DSP). Twenty-three DSP satellites orbit Earth.

Missiles use rocket engines that get very hot. The satellite has a **sensor** that can find the heat of a launched missile.

A small camera looks at the stars. The positions of the stars help the satellite determine its position.

Solar panels get light from the Sun and turn it into electricity that powers the satellite.

they fall back to Earth after their mission. Other satellites use a **space shuttle**. The space shuttle goes up like a rocket, but it lands like a plane.

Help From the Sky

Satellites are useful for many different tasks. They help armies decide on the best ground positions. Weather satellites "see" storms that are coming to help predict future conditions. **Reconnaissance** satellites have cameras. They take pictures from space of enemy territory.

Satellites use high-tech computers. They can pick up radio signals and send them a great distance. For instance, a soldier in Africa can speak with another soldier in Asia via satellite.

DID YOU KNOW?

Space is full of junk. Some of it is broken satellites and spacecraft. The junk keeps orbiting Earth. It can show up on radar. The U.S. military keeps track of it all so no one mistakes the junk for a missile attack.

▼ ANTI-SATELLITE PLANE
This U.S. F-15 fighter is carrying an anti-satellite missile. The plane flies as high as it can go. Then, it fires the missile. The missile goes much higher than any plane can. It travels into space and destroys the satellite.

Satellite Killers

Today, some countries are planning ways to destroy satellites. One way is to use "hunter-killer" satellites, or killsats. A killsat would go into orbit and hunt down another satellite. The killsat would crash into it and explode, destroying the satellite and creating more space junk.

Early Warning

Some countries, such as the United States, China, Russia, India, Pakistan, and France,

▲ COMMAND CENTER
This control room is part of the North American Aerospace Defense Command (NORAD). It is inside a mountain in Colorado. NORAD keeps track of satellites and watches for a missile attack.

▶ MISSILE LAUNCH
The LGM-30 Minuteman is an intercontinental ballistic missile (ICBM). It can hit a target on the other side of the world. This missile is being tested and does not have a bomb.

have ballistic missiles. Those missiles can travel very long distances, such as to other continents. They often carry **nuclear** bombs. Countries use satellites to watch for these missiles. The satellites warn if an attack is coming.

In the future, countries may put anti-ballistic missiles into orbit. Those weapons could shoot down enemy missiles. The United States is working on that kind of system.

DID YOU KNOW?
One kind of missile travels farther than the rest. It is called an intercontinental ballistic missile (ICBM). It can travel across an entire continent. ICBMs often carry several nuclear bombs. One ICBM can wipe out a whole city.

Advanced Space Missions

Getting satellites into space is hard. It is expensive, too. Some countries are working on less expensive ways to get satellites into orbit. One idea is to build a new space shuttle, one that will carry larger loads and fly more often.

Another plan is to build a new kind of aircraft. It is called a **spaceplane**. It will take off and land like a normal plane. But it will fly into space using rocket engines.

▼ FUTURE SPACEPLANE
U.S. scientists are working on better and less expensive ways to get into space. The X-40A is an experimental spaceplane that is part of the U.S. Air Force program. A spaceplane may replace the space shuttle.

CHAPTER 3

STEALTH TECHNOLOGY

How do you hide from the enemy? You might use **camouflage** and blend in with what is around you. Or you might make a lot of smoke, so the enemy cannot see. But what if the enemy "sees" in other ways? Radar can detect planes through smoke and clouds.

Today, militaries use **stealth** planes. Those have unique shapes and are built from special materials that are hard to detect. They are not invisible, but they are hard to locate, even with radar.

How Stealth Works

Radar sends out radio waves that bounce off objects and come back to the radar. On a radar screen, a shape appears. Stealth planes and ships stop the radio waves from bouncing back, so no information is sent.

▼ STEALTH FIGHTER
The F-22 Raptor is a modern fighter aircraft. It is designed to be very hard to spot on radar.

▲ NIGHTHAWK

The F-117 Nighthawk is even harder to detect than the Raptor. It was used by the U.S. Air Force to sneak into enemy territory and attack its targets without ever being spotted. The Nighthawk was retired in 2008.

Sneak Attack

Stealth planes sneak into enemy territory. They attack without being spotted, then sneak out again. Some stealth planes are large bombers. Others are small, fast fighters.

Stealth planes are very expensive, but they can hit targets that other planes cannot, without getting shot down. They make surprise attacks; the enemy never sees them coming!

DID YOU KNOW?

The F-22 Raptor is a U.S. stealth fighter jet. It is made of special material that absorbs radio waves so it cannot be detected. The F-22 also has angled surfaces that bounce radio waves in many directions.

▼ STEALTH SHIPS

These ships were built in Sweden. The flat panels on their sides make them very hard to spot on radar. Most ships have steel **hulls**. These ships have hulls made of plastic and **carbon fiber**. They are harder to spot than steel ships.

Stealth Missions

Attacking air defenses is difficult for normal planes, but stealth fighters can sneak up on those planes and destroy them. They clear the way for other planes to hit their targets.

Sometimes, stealth planes go on other missions. They fly deep inside enemy territory. They attack targets in enemy countries that other planes could never reach.

Hidden Ships

Warships can also "hide" from radar. They are much larger than planes, so they are harder to conceal. Radar can detect large objects much easier than smaller ones.

A ship's sharp corners and straight sides show up well on radar. To help them remain undetected, stealth ships have sloped sides. They also have smooth, rounded shapes.

Stealth Tricks

Stealth planes can "hide" in many ways. One way is to block the heat they produce. Stealth planes are also quieter than typical planes.

Pilots can also fly in ways that are undetectable. They fly very low to the ground, to avoid being detected by radar. They also fly at night.

DID YOU KNOW?

The B-2 is a U.S. stealth bomber. It is sometimes called the "Flying Wing" because of its unusual shape. It is very expensive. One plane costs more than two billion dollars to build.

▼ STEALTH BOMBER

The B-2 Spirit cannot carry as many bombs as some other planes. It also cannot fly very fast. However, it is almost invisible to radar, so it can attack targets that other planes cannot.

CHAPTER 4

MISSILE DEFENSES

Missiles are essential in modern warfare. They can travel long distances. They can search for hidden targets. They can even chase a target if it decides to run or hide.

Militaries have several ways to defend against missile attacks. They can confuse a missile so it cannot reach its target.

This crate carries four missiles. Each missile is 20 feet (6 meters) long and weighs about 2,000 lb. (907 kg). The crate tilts up to launch the missiles.

▼ PATRIOT MISSILE AIR DEFENSE SYSTEM

The U.S. Patriot Missile Air Defense System shoots down enemy planes and missiles before they reach their targets. The system includes a launcher truck, radar, and a mobile control center.

It is important to keep the launcher steady when it is firing a missile. These "legs" are put down when the truck stops. They keep it from tipping.

The Patriot launcher is mounted on a truck with oversized wheels. It moves around easily, even when off the road.

▲ PATRIOT FIRING
A U.S. Patriot missile takes off for an enemy target. Hot **exhaust** gases push the rocket out of the launcher. The launcher is open at the back so gases can escape.

Anti-Missiles

When is the best time to hit a missile? When it is still far away! Special missiles are made for this job. They are called anti-missiles. They travel long distances. They take out missiles before they can strike. Some hit enemy planes, too.

Warships also use anti-missiles. They protect themselves and other ships from attack. Some ships carry guided missiles. They can shoot down many enemy missiles at the same time.

Confusing Missiles

Using decoys is another way to defend against missile attack. Decoys are fake targets that can confuse missiles. One kind is a "hot" decoy. A heat-seeking missile will go after a hot decoy, ignoring the real target.

Another decoy tactic helps hide the target by creating a cloud of **chaff**. Chaff is tiny pieces of metal that radar cannot see through.

▼ HOT DECOYS
This helicopter is firing flares. The flares are very hot. They can confuse a heat-seeking missile. The missile will chase the flares instead of the helicopter.

At Close Range

If a missile gets close to its target, there is one last chance to stop it. Weapons that do this job are called Close-In Weapon Systems (CIWSs). Most of them are guns controlled by radar. When the radar detects the missile, the guns blast it. Sometimes, small missiles are used instead of guns.

▼ FINAL DEFENSE
The Phalanx Close-In Weapon System can save a ship by shooting down a missile. But, the system only works when the missile is less than one mile (1.6 km) away.

The Phalanx system has its own radar inside this dome. The dome protects the radar from salt water.

There is not much time to stop a missile, so the gun must destroy it quickly.

Flying Lasers

Laser guns can also stop missiles. They fire beams of light. These lasers are very powerful. They burn a missile or make it explode. They are also very large. A plane can only hold one laser. Someday, they might be small enough for soldiers to carry.

▼ **LASER PLANE**
The United States is testing a plane armed with a laser gun. It is based on a huge Boeing 747 airliner. One day, there may be smaller lasers that can fit in a fighter plane.

DID YOU KNOW?
Radar helps missiles hit their targets. But militaries can "jam," or confuse, radar. A special signal is sent out. It tricks the radar into seeing no target—or many targets. Some missiles fight back. They find the jammer and attack it.

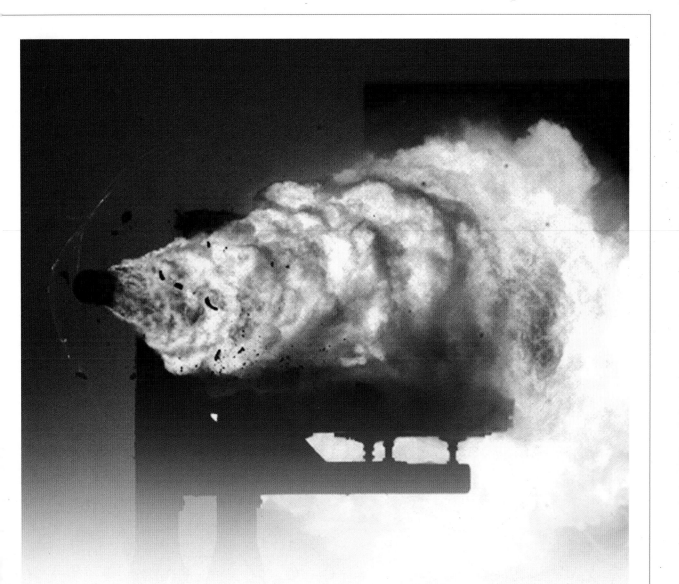

Strategic Defense

Stopping nuclear missiles is hard. But militaries are coming up with new defenses. One new weapon is the rail gun. It uses magnets and huge amounts of electrical power. It can fire a bullet much faster and farther than even the biggest regular gun.

Someday, countries may put rail guns in space. If an enemy fires nuclear missiles, rail guns will destroy them.

▲ RAIL GUN
A rail gun can fire a bullet more than three times faster than a rifle. This photo shows what the bullet looks like as it flies through the air.

CHAPTER 5

FUTURE WEAPONS

Military organizations around the world are always advancing their technology. They are constantly developing new and better weapons. Some of those weapons seem promising, but they do not all work well. Designing new weapons takes time. They have to be tested. They must be reliable.

Better Guns

The U.S. has been designing a new rifle for its soldiers, but it will probably not be ready for several years.

The new rifle can fire both bullets and small grenades. Even in the dark, soldiers can see the locations of distant targets.

The helmet has a built-in camera. It can also show maps and other data to the soldier on a tiny video screen.

▶ **FUTURE SOLDIER**
The U.S. Army is developing better equipment for foot soldiers. Those new weapons will help them do their jobs while keeping safe from enemy fire.

The rifle has a camera so the soldier can see around corners. He can shoot at the enemy while still taking cover.

IN THEIR OWN WORDS

*"[Sensors in the suit] allow us to know roughly how much energy a soldier has expended, so we know whether he's **dehydrated**, [and] whether he needs to fill his body with calories."*

Jean-Louis DeGay, Project Manager, U.S. Army Objective Force Warrior program

This soldier's suit has its own air-conditioning! A battery-powered cooling unit keeps him cool all day.

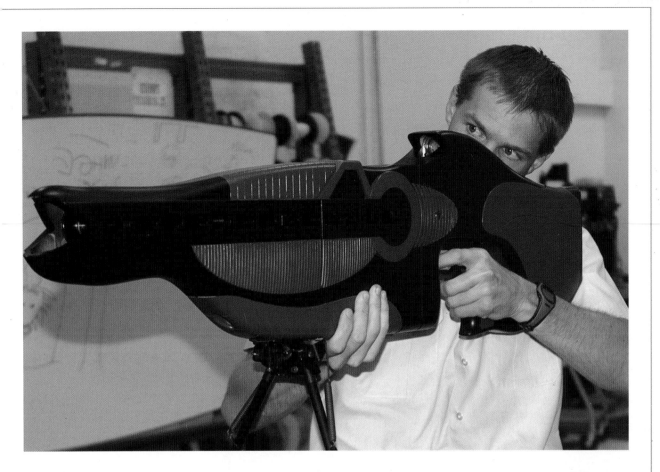

▲ LASERS, NOT BULLETS
This U.S. soldier has a set of green lasers mounted on his weapon. Instead of firing bullets, he can use bright laser beams to confuse or frighten an enemy.

Faster Firing

One company has made a new kind of gun. It is called Metal Storm. This gun can fire very fast. It has fewer moving parts than a normal weapon. It has an electrical system that fires the bullets.

Larger versions of Metal Storm are planned. They will fire grenades almost as fast as bullets. Soldiers will plug it into a laptop computer. Then, they can control the weapon from a distance.

DID YOU KNOW?
The Metal Storm gun can fire about 20,000 shots in one second. The system works, but it is not perfect. Metal Storm is not yet ready for soldiers to use in combat missions.

Robo-Soldiers

Soldiers carry heavy loads. Those loads slow them down. In the future, they may step inside a special suit. It will have a frame on the outside, called an **exoskeleton**.

That frame will let soldiers carry heavier loads. It will be powered, too. With that power, soldiers will have superhuman strength. They will be like walking tanks!

DID YOU KNOW?

Land mines shoot deadly pieces of metal in all directions. In the future, they may fire rubber stingballs. Stingballs really hurt, but they do not kill. They can be used to avoid killing innocent people.

▼ **ROBOT FIGHTER**
A soldier can carry only so much. This machine is called an exoskeleton. It will help soldiers carry their gear over long distances. It could also be used by maintenance workers loading heavy equipment such as weapons.

The exoskeleton allows the soldier to carry far heavier loads than he could without it.

Sensors detect where the soldier wants to move and give his legs extra power at just the right time.

The soldier's feet are attached to special boots that are connected to the exoskeleton. When he lifts his feet, the whole exoskeleton moves with him.

Better Protection

Soldiers of the future will be assisted by advanced weapons and equipment. Their helmets will have a GPS link and radios. Their uniforms will **monitor**, or check, their bodies. If anything is wrong, **medics** will know right away.

A special kind of armor will protect them. It is called "liquid armor." Most of the time, it is soft and flexible. If a soldier is attacked, it turns hard.

This dish sends microwaves at the enemy. They cause a burning sensation on the skin. It is so painful that enemies will run away or surrender.

The ADS is mounted on a **Humvee** so it can travel wherever it is needed.

Nonlethal Weapons

Some new weapons will be **nonlethal**. They will hurt people, but not kill them. One weapon is a special gun. It uses sound waves that make people sick. Another gun shoots pieces of plastic that knock people down.

◀ **FIGHTING WITHOUT KILLING**
The Active Denial System (ADS) developed by the U.S. military is a nonlethal weapon. It injures, but it doesn't kill anyone. ADS uses microwaves similar to those in a microwave oven to blast the enemy with heat.

GLOSSARY

camouflage—giving something the same shape or colors as its surroundings so it blends in and is hard to see

carbon fiber—strands of carbon woven together to make a material that is strong and stiff, but light

chaff—tiny pieces of metal scattered by aircraft to confuse radar

dehydrated—not having enough water

exhaust—the hot gases that come out of an engine when it burns fuel

exoskeleton—in the military, an outer body construction that is worn like a suit and provides support and protection for a soldier's inner body

Global Positioning System (GPS)—a system that helps people navigate by using satellites in space that send signals to devices on Earth

gravity—the force that pulls everything toward the center of Earth; gravity makes things fall to the ground

hulls—the main parts of ships and boats, including the sides and bottoms

Humvee—High Mobility Multipurpose Wheeled Vehicle; a U.S. military vehicle

lasers—powerful beams of light

medics—soldiers who have medical training and give first-aid to other soldiers

monitor—to check the progress or activity of something

navigation—planning and steering a route to a certain place

nonlethal—designed to slow an enemy, not kill him or her

nuclear—a type of energy created by splitting atoms of certain chemical elements

orbit—to circle around something, such as Earth

radar—a system that uses radio waves to spot things. It sends out radio waves that bounce against something and come back

reconnaissance—describes the act of discovering where enemies are located and what they are doing

sensor—a device that can pick up and send information, such as temperature

spaceplane—an aircraft that can take off and land like regular planes, but can also travel in space

space shuttle—a U.S. spacecraft that takes off like a rocket, but lands like a plane

stealth—an aircraft or ship design that is angular and hard to detect by radar or sonar

FOR MORE INFORMATION

Books

B-2 Stealth Bombers. Torque: Military Machines (series). Jack David (Children's Press, 2007)

Land Warfare of the Future. Library of Future Weaponry (series). Roderic D. Schmidt (Rosen Publishing, 2006)

Military Robots High-Tech Military Weapons (series). Steve D. White (Children's Press, 2007)

Military Technology Cool Science (series). Ron Fridell (Lerner Books, 2007)

Satellites. Exploring Space (series). David Baker and Heather Kissock (Weigl Publishers, 2008)

Stealth Attack Fighters: The F-117A Nighthawks. Michael Green and Gladys Green (Capstone Press, 2008)

U.S. Air Force Spy Planes. Blazers (series). Carrie A. Braulick (Capstone Press, 2006)

Web Sites

FCS: Brigade Combat Team
www.fcs.army.mil/systems/index.html
Examine the newest high-tech equipment that the U.S. Army is developing.

How Stuff Works: Stealth Bombers
www.science.howstuffworks.com/stealth-bomber.htm
Learn more about the B-2 bomber, see how it works, and examine photos of it.

M Ship Co: M80 Stiletto
www.mshipco.com/military_m80.html
Visit this site to see photos of a new experimental stealth ship.

The Satellite Site
www.thetech.org/exhibits/online/satellite
Discover how satellites work and even "build" a satellite.

U.S. Air Force: Technology
www.airforce.com/learn-about/technology
Click on "The Hangar" to learn about the U.S. Air Force's latest high-tech equipment, including the F-22 Raptor, a stealth fighter.

INDEX

ABOUT THE AUTHOR

Martin J. Dougherty holds a Bachelor of Education degree from the University of Sunderland in the United Kingdom. He has taught throughout northeast England and his published work includes books on subjects as diverse as space exploration, martial arts, and military hardware. He is an expert on missile systems and low-intensity warfare.